NATURAL *Golf* ®

D0568716

A LIFETIME OF

BETTER

GOLF

BY PETER FOX

Contributions by
Bob Rosburg & Chuck Hogan

GOLF DIGEST
PRODUCTIONS

Published by:

Natural Golf Corporation
2400 West Hassell Road
Hoffman Estates, IL 60195

and

Golf Digest Productions
The New York Times Company Magazine Group, Inc.
5520 Park Avenue
Trumbull, CT 06611

Book Design by Leith Chamberlain

Photography by Dom Furore, Eric Hansen,
Jim Moriarty and Stephen Szurlej

ISBN: 0-9663524-0-8

FIRST EDITION, MARCH 1998

Printed in the U.S.A.
by Cohber Press, Rochester, N.Y.

Contents

Natural Golf and Me

by Bob Rosburg

When Natural Golf asked if I would be comfortable writing and talking about the golf system it presents, I assured its people that I would be, because the Natural Golf method is very close to my way of playing.

More than that, I have seen the Natural Golf method of striking a golf ball put on awesome display by its leading practitioner, Moe Norman, under the most testing competitive circumstances anywhere—at the Masters!

When I was in my playing heyday and Moe was the reigning Canadian Amateur champion, we were paired to play in that august event's second round in April 1956. During the first round, Moe's ball striking from tee to green had been

Rosburg has seen Natural Golf up close.

truly masterful. He never missed a fairway, never missed a green. He three-putted six times: 75.

The second round was a mirror of the first. I knew then, and history has proved me correct, that I was playing in the presence of a ball-striking genius. Today you'll hear similar comments from the likes of Lee Trevino, Ken Venturi and others who you should believe and respect.

Natural Golf, Moe Norman's way, is called the most reliable swing in the game. I would find it difficult to dispute that.

It is different from the many ways of playing that fall under an umbrella of acceptance by the golf world that I will call conventional golf. Later in this book, renowned golf educator

Chuck Hogan sums up Natural Golf perfectly. Hogan says:

"When Moe Norman was competitive, the system was new, but not accepted. It will soon be accepted, but not new."

Earlier I told you that the Natural Golf way and my way are not far apart. That's true. You will learn here that there is no overlapping or interlocking grip. That's me. I always used a 10-finger grip. Natural Golf actually moves the handle out of the right-hand fingers and puts it securely in the palm. The resemblance continues in our slightly wider stances and shorter backswings.

The similarity between Moe and me goes beyond our golf swings. We're not exactly known for being subtle. That trait always seemed to get Moe in hot water. It got me a job in TV! Some guys get all the luck. And for others, it takes awhile.

So don't write the end to the Moe story. The Natural Golf people are helping to redirect his destiny. Moe is financially comfortable today. A big-time Hollywood studio is writing a movie about him, and the golf world is beginning to play and accept Natural Golf as a valid and reliable golf system.

Natural Golf arranged a reunion between Moe and me on the set of the video shoot of "A Lifetime of Better Golf." Let me say first that in my two careers I have been close to or involved with some very special golf moments. This reunion was like none of the others.

Moe Norman is undeniably a golf genius. When we played that excruciating day at Augusta, he was a kid. When we met again, he was almost like a parent: A justifiably proud, confident and authoritative figure directing his Natural Golf friends how to show a now-eager golf community his "better way to play."

Moe looked great. He was still recovering from open-heart surgery and wasn't making full swings when he masterfully demonstrated the Natural Golf method, but the unmistakable sound of his golf club striking the ball on the precise center of the clubface every time was undeniably Moe's way. It has a distinctive sound and feel. Once you do it, you will understand what I mean.

History will thank Natural Golf for preserving and promoting Moe's way. I am going to thank the company right here and now. Soon, you will, too.

The Promise of Natural Golf

by Peter Fox

I expect to shoot my age on November 17, 2008! I will be 66. If history holds, it might even happen on television.

Do you think I am kidding? I don't blame you if you do, but if you were wearing my Softspikes you would have come to understand that there is something very special about that date.

Why? For some unexplained reason, in 15-year increments something rather spectacular occurs in my life on November 17. On that date in 1993, I was introduced to Natural Golf and its famous exponent, the legendary and extraordinary Murray "Moe" Norman, who changed my golf and professional life forever. It occurred on the practice tee at Grenelefe Golf & Tennis Resort

Author Fox

outside of Orlando, Florida.

To the day 15 years earlier, November 17, 1978, at 8 p.m. to be exact, I "threw the switch" on what was the first telecast of the total sports network, ESPN. It was a pre-season basketball game between the University of Connecticut and Athletes in Action, a touring team, and I was ESPN's executive producer.

That ESPN story is for another book. This one is of Natural Golf.

So, how farfetched is shooting my age on November 17, 2008?

Consider this: "Mr. 81" was my golf nickname for decades of passionate conventional play. But today, Naturally, my scores are rarely out of the 70's and frequently at or near par with less practice—and effort. By 2008, I will be certified to play geezer tees, and the prospect of enjoying that momentous day has me eating my roughage and limiting my red meat intake.

A greater power steered me to Grenelefe's practice tee that day.

To be truthful, I was disturbed by the commotion the Natural Golf people were causing on the tee. I was trying to rehab my rusty conventional golf game. When they told me they were preparing for a Moe Norman Clinic later, I'm embarrassed to admit, I asked, "Just who the hell is Moe Norman?"

A newsman's curiosity prevailed, however, and I half listened to a Natural Golf zealot while watching golf's Forrest Gump—Moe—strike balls in a manner that astounded me. I was duly impressed by Moe's unfailing accuracy and laser-like ball flight. Moreover, I was overwhelmed by the unique and repeating sound of the ball being struck by the precise center of his golf club every time.

Today, that sound inspires me. It inspires because even I can attain it on a more than occasional basis. Along with it come the accuracy and distance that make for more fairways, greens, pars and birdies. Better golf, plain and simple.

I didn't know then—but do now—that Moe Norman's and Natural Golf's method of striking the ball was what made it all possible. I didn't know then—but do now—that Moe Norman and Natural Golf would affect my life so deeply. The Natural Golf and Moe Norman way is refreshingly simple. It is easy to understand and perform. It produces strong, straight shots and happy golfers.

My curiosity ultimately led me to Larry Olson, president of Natural Golf Corporation, who took my criticism of his company's communication materials to heart and invited me to help Natural Golf improve its teaching tools.

Phase one of that process was to film Moe Norman's golf swing in an environment that would allow a sophisticated analysis on video. I'll confess to being somewhat intimidated by Moe's demeanor the day we gathered at Pine Needles in North Carolina.

In preparation I had learned that Lee Trevino called Moe Norman the best ball striker ever to play golf and that Ken Venturi nicknamed him "Pipeline Moe," describing his remarkable accuracy. I learned that the likes of Sam Snead,

"To me, the name Natural Golf is perfect. It's a natural motion."

—William Stanton, New York

Ben Hogan, Nick Faldo, Nick Price, Fred Couples and Ben Crenshaw had studied his magnificent move.

I learned, too, that Moe's often erratic behavior had kept him in relative golf obscurity. Moe Norman that day seemed grumpy, wary and distant, but altogether, pretty together. I was absolutely unprepared for the eloquent virtual monologue that he put on for Natural Golf's cameras after dinner in a fireside chat in the golf-rich vestibule of the main building at Pine Needles Lodge and Golf Club.

Over the course of an hour or more, Moe chronicled his life and his golf in a frank and touching way that moved me to tears. Those historic moments became the basis for *Golf Digest*'s popular video "Moe Norman and Natural Golf."

Moe's way is Natural Golf's way and vice versa. Moe Norman continues to play an active role in influencing the design of Natural Golf equipment and materials. In a recent interview, Moe said of Natural Golf:

"My way is so different only one outfit in the whole world can teach it. Others think they know it, but they don't, because they never came to me."

For the sake of historical accuracy, you should understand that Moe developed his method intuitively; he began playing that way in 1943 when he was 14 and a caddie in Kitchener, Ontario, Canada, his home.

Natural Golf developed a ball-striking method that is fundamentally similar to Moe Norman's method. The Natural Golf System explains why Moe's unconventional method is so very successful. Time and Natural Golf's inevitable growth will support that.

Early Natural Golf work—manuals and videos—were heavy with scientific explanations and overly technical directions on how to perform the Natural Golf motion.

Over time, the practical application of those science-laden learning tools proved to be much too complicated for the vast majority of people to apply in the process of learning our very simple and more effective Natural Golf System.

This work, *A Lifetime of Better Golf*, comprises successful field-tested and easy-to-understand presentations of the Natural Golf System.

In it, we promise to show you how to play golf better—Naturally. That is Natural Golf's basic promise: better golf.

We'll make some other promises to you along the way. They will be promises we can keep. Kept promises inspire loyalty, and Natural Golf knows it must earn yours.

One of our first promises is to refrain from the outlandish hype that has come to be a hallmark of golf-product introductions in recent times. You'll find no shaky claims of 300-yard drives and 10-minute or 10-day, 10-stroke handicap reductions. We will document some major improvements made by Natural Golf students.

When we asked Golf Digest Productions to assist us in preparing this instructional material, one of the requirements was that we allow its staffers, who have worked closely on instruction books and videos with the editors of *Golf Digest*, to exert quality control over the material.

It was easy for Natural Golf to agree to those terms, knowing that those editors, intimately familiar with the way *Golf Digest* presents its instruction material, would improve the quality of Natural Golf's own instruction material. Indeed, Natural Golf likes to think that this expert presentation will further instill consumer confidence in its validity.

In fact, validity is exactly what Golf Digest Schools teaching professional John Elliott referred to in his closing narrative statement on the "Moe Norman and Natural Golf" video. Elliott said, "Showing you why Natural Golf is a valid way to consider golfing was my duty as a responsible golf professional."

Learning to play the Natural Golf System is a process. It's a process that we are confident will produce better golf for you. It will take time—30 to 90 days at least—and it requires a commitment, instruction, practice and proper equipment.

Our confidence to promise better golf comes from thousands of hours of teaching the Natural Golf method. Our successes with players of all levels, genders and ages allow us to confidently and resolutely pledge to refund your investment in Natural Golf if you are not satisfied that we have met our commitment to you.

Along the way in this book, we will share with you learning experiences of Natural Golfers who are enjoying golf successes with our system. Their remarks are genuine and are quoted directly from the recorded interviews of a journalist-researcher we asked to gather authentic Natural Golf comments and critiques

The author watches Moe Norman.

from real Natural Golfers.

Now, after all that talk of how promising Natural Golf is and the promises Natural Golf will keep with its players, we will make you a promise:

We promise that this next phrase—single axis—is the most complicated one we will use in this Natural Golf primer.

When we show you how to hold a golf club in a single axis—or what we like to call a Straight Line configuration—and let you swat golf balls from that setup position, you will hit them straighter and longer more often than you would from the conventional golf way, which is a two-axis method.

We have tried to boil Natural Golf down to ordinary language. We have learned that if we keep it simple, more people "get it" and enjoy its benefits.

Science was the premise from which Natural Golf was conceived, and there are people in its hierarchy who are well-versed in it. If you absolutely, positively must have a physics, kinesiology, neuroscience and biomechanic blabfest before taking a Natural Golf baby step, you will be able to fill that need. It won't happen in the context of *A Lifetime of Better Golf*, however.

Making Natural Golf education user-friendly has been a subject of a substantial effort, led primarily by Moe Norman with Natural Golf's leading practitioners.

Ken Ellsworth, a PGA Tour veteran and Natural Golf's Director of Instruction, and Todd Graves, Moe Norman's protégé whom the golfing press nicknamed "Little Moe" while he competed on the Canadian PGA Tour, led the effort to streamline the instruction. And, of course, *Golf Digest*'s instruction features on

Moe Norman and Natural Golf in the December 1995 issue had major influence on the presentation of our information.

Natural Golf is pleased to include a section in this book by noted golf coach Chuck Hogan. He advises Natural Golfers how to take what Moe Norman calls, "the longest walk in golf—from the practice tee to the first tee."

Hogan has coached such tour pros as Peter Jacobsen, Colleen Walker, John Cook, Johnny Miller, Raymond Floyd, Duffy Waldorf, David Ogrin and Cindy Rarick. He is the founder of Sports Learning and Performance, and his programs blend the mental and physical aspects of golf instruction.

For me, the opportunity to share the joy of discovering an easier and better way to play golf with anyone who will pay attention seems to be my destiny—at least for the remainder of these next 15 years or so.

I wonder, though: After that November 17, 2008, six-under-par, age-shooting performance (with appropriate apologies to Peggy Lee and composers Jerry Leiber and Mike Stoller), will I ask:

"Is that all there is?"

I doubt it.

I'll probably have to get a real job.

WHY PLAY GOLF?

Golf writers of distinguished pedigree have waxed poetic about the glories of this royal and ancient game. Henry Longhurst, Herbert Warren Wind, Michael Murphy, Red Smith and David Owen have all written eloquently about golf's great challenge and thrill.

If you play golf, you know its subtleties and its vagaries. You also know the spellbinding influence golf holds over its practitioners. If you are a golfer, there is no need to explain it.

You and your comrades-in-the-game share a language, a lifestyle and even a literature that pleasantly blend tests of character with flights of fancy and moments of madness.

If you are not a golfer, you need to make friends with one and listen to that golfer with an open heart. You will be introduced to a romantic game, an exercise of intellect, spirit and body, a pastime that promises to always quench your thirst for fun and sport for the rest of your active life.

Natural Golf, we believe, can enhance the experience.

WHY PLAY NATURAL GOLF?

SQUARE TRACKING

5-IRON

DRIVER

The Natural Golf swing is easy to make. And its rewards come quickly.

When you compare various golf swings carefully, you can see why the Natural Golf swing is simple and easy to do. The Natural Golf swing eliminates or reduces several movements.

How? With its Natural Palm Grip, its Straight Line Setup and its Straight Line Motion, all of which result in its unique Square Tracking action. Unlike many "easier, convenient and streamlined" new concepts, however, with the Natural Golf System, you must accept *no* compromise of quality or performance as a tradeoff for its ease.

Natural Golfers come to experience just the opposite, in fact. *Better* ball striking—leading to improved accuracy and distance—is what Natural Golfers say is the primary benefit of the Natural Golf System. And more properly struck and accurate long and short golf shots produce better golf scores.

Whether you are new to golf or just new to Natural Golf, this better ball striking will be obvious when you execute a correct Natural

There is a dramatic reduction of clubface rotation in Natural Golf's Square Tracking path, shown here with a 5-iron and a driver. The result is greater clubhead extension down the target line, creating strong, straight shots.

Golf swing.

Once you make the simpler Natural Golf basic motion and learn to repeat it, you then will experience another benefit that current Natural Golfers describe as our "low maintenance" feature. Because you need to precisely coordinate fewer body and equipment movements, your need for constant, continual rehearsal of the swing is reduced.

In other words, with Natural Golf, less practice generally is required to maintain a level of playing excellence. Of course, more practice makes for more improvement.

Another strong benefit of playing Natural Golf's simpler system is that it appears to extend the playing careers of many golfers. Natural Golf believes its swing puts less stress on a number of body parts. The result: more players being able to take up the sport and stay in it. Natural Golfers with back problems report the most benefit, although players inhibited by arthritic conditions are equally enthusiastic.

The promise of Natural Golf excites most golfers who experience its better ball striking with less effort. The question that necessarily follows is, compared to what? The answer to that question is: compared to conventional golf.

While we do not paint the conventional golf swing as wrong, bad or otherwise inferior to Natural Golf's, we do assert that it is more complicated to perform than Natural Golf's streamlined striking motion.

There are more moving parts to get out of sync in the conventional swing, and therein lies the advantage of Natural Golf.

> "I think it is a very good, sound way to play. It doesn't require the critical timing that the conventional golf swing does."
>
> —Jerry Fulton, Mississippi

Conventional golf, as we define it, is any golf method in which the grip, or handle, of the club is placed in the fingers of the right hand. In that definition we include what is commonly known as the overlapping grip, the interlocking finger grip and even the not uncommon 10-finger grip.

The most popular grip today is the overlapping grip, also known as the Vardon Grip. The Vardon era, as it has come to be known in golf circles, began 50 years before Moe Norman was born and 64 years before he intuitively chose *not* to employ British champion Harry Vardon's conventional positioning of the club handle in the fingers of the hands.

Vardon, like Moe Norman, would not accept the golf conventions of his time, which placed the grip of the club in the hands, much like baseball players hold a bat today. Vardon put the grip in the fingers and joined the two hands by overlapping the index finger of his left hand with the pinkie of his right.

However, with the club held in the fingers of the right hand, it is extremely difficult—if not impossible—for a conventional golfer to align the grip, or handle, of the golf club with the right forearm the way Natural Golfers do. To accomplish that desired Straight Line relationship between the grip, or handle, and the forearm, the conventional golfer rotates the forearms, which has the effect of turning the

The handle rests in the fingers of the right hand of a conventional grip (A).

The handle does not align with the forearm in a conventional grip (B).

CONVENTIONAL SWING 1

CONVENTIONAL GRIP A

2

3

B

face of the club off of a square relationship to the swing path as he makes his backswing.

On the way back toward the ball, in the downswing, the conventional golfer has an urgent need to rotate the hands and arms again, this time in the opposite direction, to return the face of the club to a position as close as possible to its square starting position. Making the task even harder is the speed that the head of the club travels as it approaches impact with the ball—often between 75 and 100 miles an hour.

To further complicate matters, reliable golf studies show that a *maximum* of only two degrees of clubface variation off a purely

The forearm rotation in the conventional golfer's backswing causes the club to swing on multiple planes (1).

At the top, the clubface, hands, arms, shoulders, torso and hips all have rotated considerably (2).

In photo 3, the clubface, hands, arms, shoulders, torso and hips all return to square ever so briefly at impact in the conventional swing, then rotate the other way.

1

2

Because of conventional golf's two-axis setup (1), the conventional golfer's spine moves up and away so he can extend and straighten his arms at impact (2).

the hips, torso and shoulders rotate away from that same line, making the move extremely complicated and difficult to repeat reliably.

Furthermore, during the downswing the conventional golfer must strive to reduce the angle between the handle of the club and the right forearm that was created at the beginning of the swing by the finger grip. The conventional golfer does this by actually moving the spine upward and backward, away from the ball, in an effort to reach impact in the pure Straight Line relationship between the right forearm and the club's grip that the Natural Golf Setup allows.

If the conventional golfer doesn't make the "up and away" spine movement while the arms are attempting to extend and straighten at impact, he will likely contact the turf before the ball and hit a poor, weak, "fat" shot. Overdoing the move causes a skulled or thinned shot.

Natural Golfers are different. But casual observers can easily miss the visually subtle, but effectively dramatic point of difference in the Natural Golf Setup: The single Straight Line the right forearm creates in its relationship with the handle of the club when you use the Natural Palm Grip.

This straight line—or single axis—allows the Natural Golfer to make Natural Golf's totally unique move, called Straight Line Motion.

Natural Golf's Straight Line Motion dramatically reduces the rotation of the clubface and allows for greater clubhead extension down the target line. The result is what Natural Golf calls Square Tracking. It is this innovation that

square position is needed to allow a golfer to hit a golf ball into a 40-yard wide landing area, 200 yards away from the spot where it was struck. That is a narrow margin of error. The effects of aim and weather elements are not included.

In a conventional golf swing, not only do the hands and arms rotate the club's face off, on and off the intended line of ball flight, but also

"When the pro went through the science of single axis vs. two axis, it just made sense to me that there was less to go wrong with the Natural Golf swing. Immediately, I hit the ball solid."

—David Coon, Texas

creates strong, straight Natural Golf shots.

The Natural Golfer experiences little or no need to rotate the hands, arms, hips, torso and shoulders during the instant of impact with the ball.

Nor does the Natural Golfer have to move the spine "up and away" because, from the start, the arms are extended in the desired Straight Line impact position.

Natural Golf's ideal position at impact has the golfer's hips, torso and shoulders close to facing, or exactly parallel to, an imaginary line drawn back from the intended target through the original position of the golf ball.

Both feet are in solid contact with the ground. That solid feeling produces "quiet hips," a reduced hip rotation that is the key to Natural Golf's only moving fundamental—facing the ball at impact. The resulting balance allows the Natural Golfer to make a confident, strong striking motion.

That confidence translates quickly into distance. Subconsciously, the Natural Golfer's internal Power Dial turns itself up because the golfer is certain the club is on a path that will propel the ball in a safe and playable direction.

The promise of Natural Golf manifests itself best in the confidence Natural Golfers have that their shots will be solid and accurate. They spend a brief amount of time addressing the ball, they make a simple Straight Line Motion and their shots fly true to the target. Then they spend a lot of time enjoying the results.

The promise of Natural Golf takes on credibility as it is experienced.

Better ball striking. Better scoring. More fun. Less strain.

Supernatural? No.

Promising? Yes.

So, why play Natural Golf?

Because it can result in A Lifetime of Better Golf.

With Natural Golf's Straight Line, one-axis setup (3), the Natural Golfer's extended, straight-arm impact position (4) matches his address position.

The First
NATURAL
GOLFER

The performance of the first Natural Golfer—Moe Norman—is testament to the validity of the method.

By dictionary definition, Murray "Moe" Norman is a phenomenon. He is unique, independent, proud and excruciatingly withdrawn, probably as a result of early life traumas and character maulings he suffered from golf power brokers in his native Canada.

By workaday world definition, he is a very nice man, humbly aware of his special gift, and though not given to flaunting it, he is justifiably proud to put it on precise and repeatable display.

Moe Norman, golf professional, is quite simply the best striker of a golf ball in the game. Sam Snead and Lee Trevino have

> ## "I'm lucky. I've got a talent. I can explain it and I can show it to people, which is what I love doing." —Moe Norman

openly said as much, and Ben Hogan indirectly said the same.

Ken Venturi, who knows as much about the art and science of ball striking as anyone, coined the nickname "Pipeline Moe" in describing Moe's infallible accuracy.

One day in the 1950's, Moe and Hogan were on the practice tee together at a pro tournament when a spectator asked Hogan to take a look at Moe. Hogan believed any ball hit dead straight was an accident.

After each of the first six balls he watched Moe hit, Hogan said, "Accident." After watching Moe hit several more, Hogan said: "Just keep hitting those accidents, kid."

Trevino, in a televised interview, said of Moe: "I don't know of any player, ever, who could strike a golf ball like Moe Norman, as far as hitting it solid, knowing where it is going and knowing what he wants to do with the ball. Moe Norman is a genius when it comes to playing the game of golf."

Those men saw Moe at his best—in his prime—when he was on his way to shooting more than 40 course records. Three of them are scores of 59, shot in competition.

As he nears his 70th year, Moe Norman continues to strike golf shots, with any club from the wedge to the driver, on a dead-straight line to his target.

He inspires Natural Golf and aspiring Natural Golfers.

Moe Norman, the best ball striker ever.

HOW TO PLAY
NATURAL GOLF

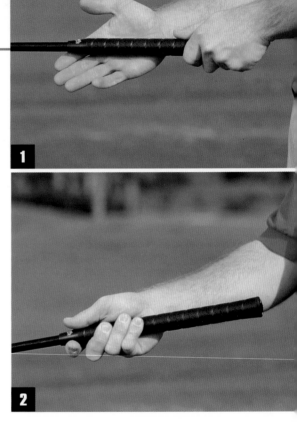

1

2

Golf is a difficult game to play. Natural Golf simplifies it.

The Natural Golf System's swing has fewer moving parts and angles than conventional golf's.

Its simplicity regularly produces strong, straight shots.

Natural Golf teaches its method in four simple parts.

They are:

- How to hold the club.
- How to stand with the club at the ball.
- How to move as you swing the club.
- How to think while you are swinging.

HOW TO HOLD THE CLUB

The handle runs across the second knuckle of the index finger, through the palm and across the top of the heel pad of the right hand (1-2).

Holding the club is the single most basic element of golf.

Because the club moves the ball and the hands move the golf club it is easy to understand why so much instructional emphasis is put on the way you hold or grip the club.

It is Natural Golf's first fundamental—the Natural Palm Grip—that makes playing golf so much easier for the Natural Golfer. Not only does the Natural Palm Grip make golf easier to play, but it makes you play *better* golf, too. The Natural Palm Grip is the foundation of Natural Golf's Straight Line Setup, Straight Line Motion and Square Tracking path, which consistently deliver a square clubface to the ball at impact.

One note: The Natural Palm Grip works best with clubs with handles that are thicker

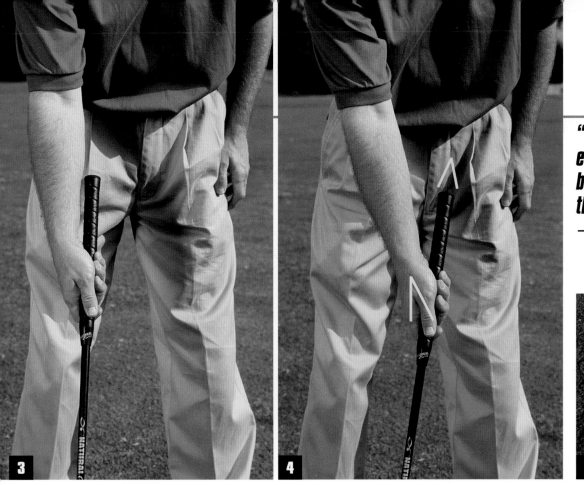

3

4

5

than normal and are untapered *(see page 74)*. When a Natural Golfer plays with conventional, narrow, tapered handles, he may feel as if the clubhead is twisting off square at contact. Inadvertently, he may also have a tendency to allow the handle to go back to being held in the fingers rather than keeping it in the palm.

Right hand

Here is how you hold the club in your right hand for the Natural Palm Grip:

Place the handle of the club across the second knuckle of the index finger and on the heel pad of the hand so that the handle lies diagonally across the palm. The "V" formed by the thumb and index finger should point between your right cheek and right shoulder when the hands are at body center.

Now move the butt end of the club slightly away from the right forearm so it points in the direction of the left shoulder.

Move the butt of the handle away from the forearm so it points at the left shoulder and so the thumb-forefinger "V" points between the right cheek and right shoulder (3-4).

How the Natural Golfer sees his right-hand grip (5).

Left hand & hands together

Here is how you hold the club in your left hand:

Place the handle of the club across the second knuckle of the index finger and on the heel pad of the hand. The "V" formed by the thumb and index finger should point between your right cheek and right shoulder when the hands are at body center. Place the left thumb slightly right of the centerline of the grip of the club.

Together, the right and left hands on the club form the Natural Palm Grip.

A couple of notes of caution: First, the Natural Palm Grip is the way to hold a golf club. Do not mistake it for the way a baseball player holds a bat in the palms. Second, when you squeeze the handle of the club too tightly, you create muscle tension in the arms and shoulders. That tension interferes with well-coordinated golf swings. Natural Golf discourages you from gripping too tightly.

In fact, successful Natural Golfers—including Moe Norman—say they consciously apply some grip pressure with the left hand, especially in the last three fingers, and are aware of light or no grip pressure in the right hand.

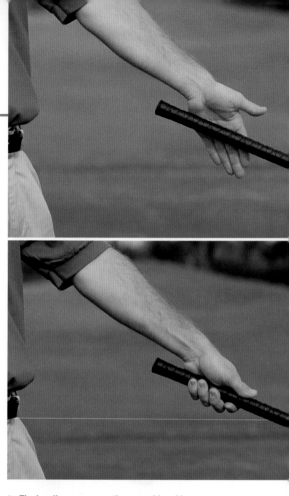

The handle runs across the second knuckle of the index finger and the heel pad of the left hand (above).

The thumb-forefinger "V" of the left hand points between the right cheek and right shoulder, and the thumb is slightly right of the centerline (1).

How the Natural Golfer sees his left-hand grip (2).

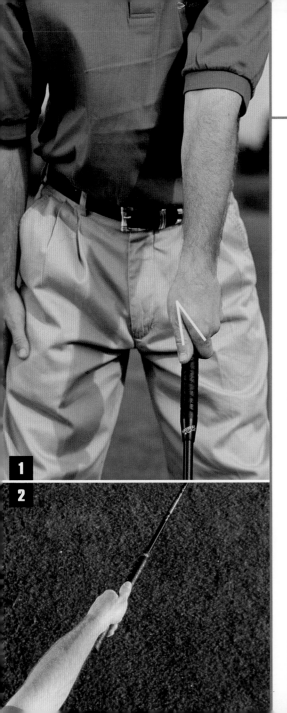

1

2

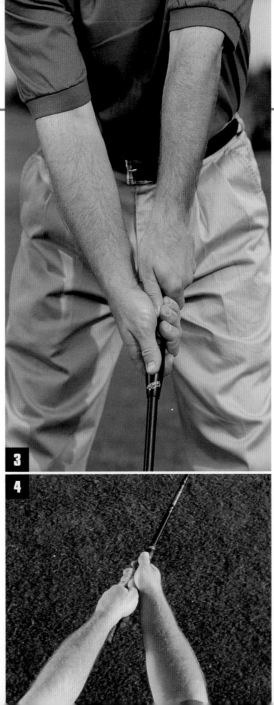

3

4

The full Natural Palm Grip (3) and how the Natural Golfer sees it (4). Note how the palms are facing each other.

Straight Line relationship

In some ways, the Natural Palm Grip resembles its conventional counterparts, the different finger grips. The dramatic difference is hard to see from a face-on perspective, but when viewed from the perspective of looking down the target line, the Natural Golf Straight Line Setup is easily differentiated from the two-line conventional setup.

To repeat: The Straight Line relationship between the grip of the golf club and the right arm is the absolute foundation of the Natural Golf System. It produces a clubface path that Natural Golf calls Square Tracking, which consistently delivers a square clubface to the ball at impact.

The Straight Line Setup, made possible by the Natural Palm Grip, enables Natural Golf's Square Tracking of the clubface to occur.

The Straight Line relationship between the handle and forearm is the foundation of the Natural Golf System and produces Natural Golf's Square Tracking clubface swing path.

> *"The palm grip—being able to grab the club and haul off and whack the ball and feel confident that you are going to make solid contact—was real helpful to me."*
>
> —Bo Yoder, Maine

CONVENTIONAL

The two-line setup of conventional finger grips makes Square Tracking extremely difficult, if not impossible.

The Straight Line grasping of the golf club's grip inspired Natural Golf's name.

Bell ringers, tug-of-war contestants, fencers, painters, carpenters, javelin throwers, fishermen, marksmen, lecturers, lacrosse players and lumberjacks, to name a few, all quite naturally hold the "tools of their trade" in the efficient Straight Line way a Natural Golfer holds a golf club.

Unlike the conventional grip's two-axis relationship (above), the butt of the handle is invisible in the Natural Palm Grip and the single-axis, Straight Line Setup (left).

HOW TO STAND WITH THE CLUB AT THE BALL

5-IRON

Feet

The Natural Golfer places the feet farther apart than most conventional players. How wide you place your feet may vary, depending on the length of the club you are swinging. The longer the club, the wider your stance should be.

The purpose of the wider stance is to encourage balance and limit hip rotation.

Natural Golf's Straight Line striking motion gives you confidence that you'll strike the ball squarely. As a result, your hands and arms tend to move through the hitting area strongly. The better balance of the wider stance provides stability for that strong striking motion.

You should place the insides of your feet shoulder-width apart when using a 5-iron. They should be slightly farther apart for longer clubs and slightly closer together for shorter clubs. Your height, weight and body proportions may influence slight stance adjustments from these guidelines. Taller, longer-legged Natural Golfers tend to have wider stances than Natural Golfers of average or shorter statures.

As a Natural Golfer, you have the option of placing the feet so that the toes point either directly at the target line or are turned slightly off of it. The more the feet are turned away from the target line, the greater the tendency for hip rotation.

Feet square to target line

The toes can either point at the target line (above) or be turned slightly off it (below).

Feet turned off target line

The insides of the feet are about as wide as the outsides of the shoulders for a 5-iron.

DRIVER

The right heel stays on the ground during impact.

"I knocked about three strokes off my handicap this summer. I find that using the method, I do hit the ball squarer, more than I ever did."

—Bob Ralston, Massachusetts

How to Play: Stance

Posture

Once you get the feet placed properly, turn your attention to body posture. Tilt your spine at an angle that encourages Natural Golf's Straight Line arm extension. This "high hands" posture produces Natural Golf's Square Tracking path.

The angle of the arm extension will vary. It is affected by the length of the club. The shorter the club is, the closer you will be to the ball and the more upright the angle should be between the arms and the body.

Distribute your weight evenly between the heels and balls of the feet. Balance your weight evenly between your left foot and right foot. Many successful Natural Golfers, including Moe Norman, keep their "flat feet" very quiet and in full contact with the ground well through the club's impact with the ball.

5-IRON

WEDGE

Tilt the spine from the hips to encourage the arm extension and high hands of Natural Golf's Straight Line Setup with a driver, 5-iron and wedge. The shorter the club, the closer your feet are to the ball and the more upright your arm-extension angle is.

WEDGE

5-IRON

Hands, clubhead & ball

How you position the hands in the Natural Golf Straight Line Setup and how that affects the clubhead's relationship to the ball are unique to Natural Golf.

First, in the Natural Golf System you position your hands in the center of the body with all clubs.

Second, in the Natural Golf System you position the clubhead away from the ball. Why? The Natural Golf clubhead position allows you to start the backswing on the proper path and insures that the clubhead behind the bottom of the swing's arc, as should be. How do you create that unique position? With the hands body-centered

30

DRIVER

the handle of the golf club away from the right forearm with a very slight backward movement of the right wrist.

Golf language calls it "loading" or "cocking." Kinesiologists call it extension.

Once again, the length of the shaft of the club affects the setup. With the hands body-centered and the butt end of the handle pointing toward the left shoulder, the clubhead of a driver will set farther away from the ball than the clubhead of a wedge, and the lengths of the shafts of the other clubs will set their clubheads between those extremes.

Also affecting the distance between the ball and the clubhead is the position of the ball itself in relation to the golfer's body. In the Natural Golf System, you position the ball in relation to your body rather than your feet.

For wedges and short irons, play the ball in front of your body center. For the driver, fairway woods and long irons, play the ball in front of your left hip or shoulder.

For other clubs, play the ball between those ball-position guidelines.

Now you know three of Natural Golf's four unique swing basics:

1. The Natural Palm Grip.
2. Natural Golf's Straight Line relationship between the right arm and handle of the club.
3. Natural Golf's slightly wider and more stable stance.

You're almost Naturalized.

"I don't get in trouble like I used to. I don't have to think about the game as much as you do with the other swing."

—Elaine Perlin, Virginia

the Natural Palm Grip, you point the butt end of the handle of the club toward the left shoulder. That creates another Natural Golf Straight Line extending from the clubhead, along the shaft, through the hands, up the left arm toward the left shoulder.

Successful Natural Golfers, including Moe Norman, achieve this position by pushing

How to Play: Swing

HOW TO MOVE AS YOU SWING

The fourth Natural Golf swing basic is the only one that relates to movement: facing the ball when the clubface contacts the ball.

That is a significant departure from conventional golf.

Facing the ball at impact promotes Natural Golf's Square Tracking path of the clubface through the impact area. Square Tracking requires considerably less leg, hip, torso and arm rotation than conventional golf.

The conventional golfer rotates the legs and hips from on the target line to off it, then back on it and finally off it again. All that body rotation is necessary to allow the "crossover" movement of the golfer's simultaneously rotating arms and hands in an effort to return the club's face to a square position as it hits the ball.

When you face the ball at impact using a Natural Golf swing, your body transfers energy to the ball in the direction you want the ball to fly. This contributes to strong, straight Natural Golf ball flight.

A face-on, high-speed look at the Natural Golf swing

Natural Golf's Todd Graves hits a 5-iron.

1

2

6 IMPACT WITH A 5-IRON

IMPACT WITH A WEDGE

IMPACT WITH A DRIVER

Facing the ball at impact.

Hands are no higher than shoulders at the top.

3

4

5

7

8

9

Square Tracking begins.

A down-the-line, high-speed look at the Natural Golf swing

Natural Golf's Director of Instruction and PGA Tour veteran Ken Ellsworth hits a 5-iron.

1

2

6 IMPACT WITH A 5-IRON

Right heel on the ground during impact.

IMPACT WITH A WEDGE

IMPACT WITH A DRIVER

Backswing

The Natural Golf full-swing movements that precede and follow the face-the-ball-at-impact position are economical, too.

Begin the backswing with a turn of the left shoulder, moving the arms rearward as the right arm folds. Keep your hands relaxed so they can "load energy" for the hitting action—by extending or cocking—without conscious effort. The hands don't move past shoulder height at the top of the Natural Golf backswing.

The Natural Golf top-of-the-swing hitting position may be a familiar arm-hand position for you. It resembles the "top-of-the-swing" position of activities such as hammering, throwing and hitchhiking.

In the Natural Golf System, the left and right shoulders *operate independently of each other.* The left turns approximately 90 degrees from its starting position, while the right only turns about 45 degrees.

Check your position at the top of your backswing. The left arm should not bend noticeably at the elbow and the left shoulder should be under the chin.

Turn the left shoulder and extend the arms rearward to begin the backswing (1). At the top of backswing, the hands are at shoulder height (2). The left shoulder has turned approximately 90 degrees, the right about 45 degrees (3).

"*I would like to take new young players and use the method to introduce them to the game of golf. The whole thing seems so uncomplicated.*"

—Jesse Bishop, North Carolina

Note that the clubface, at the top of the swing, is pointing more toward the sky than on a conventional swing, indicating less clubface rotation. Also the angle of the right leg doesn't change—there's no sway— a direct result of the wide stance.

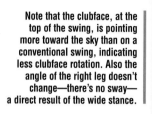

45°

90°

Downswing

The downswing is simply a downward movement of the right elbow that takes the right hand and arm away from the right shoulder and moves the elbow in front of the right hip.

Many successful Natural Golfers, including Moe Norman, accomplish this with a conventional golf feeling that the *left arm* is initiating the action, that the left arm is pulling the right elbow, hand and arm into the right elbow's proper position in front of the right hip.

Whether you accomplish this move with a "feeling" from the left side or with a motion that originates from the right side, it is important that the arms get in front of the right hip prior to any substantial movement of that hip.

"I like the whole method: the grip, the stance, keeping the right foot down through impact, facing the ball. I find I get more solid contact and better accuracy. I'm also getting more distance."

—Ray McLeod, New Jersey

Move the right elbow in front of the right hip on the down-swing.

Impact

During the downswing, the weight of the club-head will encourage a "loading" of energy in your right hand. That loading creates an even greater angle at the right wrist hinge. Retain the angle until it straightens through the impact area. Your folded right arm simply straightens through the impact area.

The release of the right wrist angle during the instant of impact occurs naturally. Any conscious effort by you to affect the timing of that right hand release will usually result in a poor shot.

Those successful Natural Golfers who say they feel they are consciously pulling with the left arms likely inhibit the brain's ability to consciously interfere with the natural release of the stored energy in the right hand and arm.

During impact your hips stabilize on the desired square-to-the-ball flight line. They do slide slightly—but powerfully. The hips are close to parallel to the desired line, as your weight shifts forward along it. The weight shift is coordinated with the momentum you've created by swinging your arms and club. The head, at impact, is over the right knee.

Your right heel remaining on the ground allows your hips to stay nearly square until the ball has left the club and is well on its way toward its target. The way your right heel remains in contact with the ground at impact is a distinct Natural Golf trait. It is virtually impossible for you to keep the right heel in contact with the ground if your hips rotate well off the square relationship with the target line.

> "You realize you don't have to have great power. It is a natural short swing with a lot of leverage."
>
> —Mike Boulas, Michigan

1

A loading of energy in the right hand will increase the wrist-hinge angle just before impact (1). That energy naturally releases at impact, as the right heel stays down (2). The right arm naturally straightens by the time the club reaches the end of the impact area (3). Note how the head is over the right knee.

Finish

Once the ball has left the clubface, the Natural Golf shot is technically over. As that occurs, you should find that both your arms are fully extended. The clubhead in a Natural Golf swing usually will extend farther along the target line than in a conventional swing.

An instant later, the tension created by the momentum of your movement releases. Your arms and hips rotate, your weight transfers off the right foot onto the left, and your torso turns toward the target.

That's it. Those are the mechanical basics.

After impact, both arms fully extend down the target line. As tension releases, your arms and hips rotate, your weight transfers to the left foot and your torso turns (1), producing a high finish (2).

> *"I went from a 21 down to a 15 this season. I won the most-improved golfer award at my home course up in Minneapolis."* —Col. Richard Kennison, Florida

2

HOW TO THINK AS YOU SWING

> "What I like about it is that I have confidence now. When I go and tee up a ball I know I am going to hit it. I'm not going to dub it."
>
> —Jack Sherman, Florida

There's one more segment of the Natural Golf System teaching method. Like other Natural Golf fundamentals, it is pretty easy—a no brainer, so to speak!

Natural Golf staunchly insists that you empty your conscious mind of mechanical details of how to strike the golf ball while actually playing the game.

Conscious thinking about details of the Natural Golf swing during the motion is bad. It produces poor shots and unhappy golfers. Good Natural Golfers think mostly about the target, and perhaps about the shape of the arc of the ball's flight, while they are swinging.

There is a bookshelf full of nerve science that tells you why lists of conscious swing thoughts destroy smooth performance. Instead, you should trust your subconscious mind to enable you to swing smoothly.

In fact, if you don't mess with it, your subconscious will repeat the same good motion virtually every time.

One of the real benefits of choosing to play the Natural Golf System is that it is so streamlined. As a Natural Golfer, you really don't have many mechanics to think about. That simplicity encourages a subconscious ideal performance of the motion.

It is our experience that new Natural Golfers quickly come to trust that they can make consistent and predictable contact with the ball with little conscious effort.

When that occurs, a Natural Golfer is born.

The Natural Golfer
avoids conscious
thinking about mechanics
during the swing.

LEARNING NATURAL GOLF

We nurture all new Natural Golfers with a graduated learning process.

It does not matter if you are an accomplished conventional golfer or a beginner. In formal instruction environments, we insist on introducing the Natural Golf fundamentals in this way. We urge you to follow it as prescribed in the following drills.

Horizontal drill

The first learning exercise is our "horizontal" drill, a four-stage drill that introduces you to the Natural Golf movement.

The first stage has four steps: 1) Hold the club horizontally in front of your face with the right hand, using the right-hand Natural Palm Grip. 2) Add the left hand to the grip. 3) Turn your left arm and shoulder while folding your right elbow. 4) Return your arms to the starting position, so the right arm straightens.

The second stage repeats the steps of the first stage, but you tilt the angle of your spine slightly and suspend the head of the club between horizontal and the ground.

The third stage repeats the second, but you tilt the angle of the spine more, until you ground the head of the club behind a tee marking where a ball will be in the next stage.

In the first stage, hold the club horizontally in front of your face with the right hand in the Straight Line relationship (1), shown here to the side for demonstration purposes. Add the left hand (2), turn the left arm and shoulder while folding the right elbow (3), then return to a straight-arm position (4).

First Stage

1   2   3   4

The fourth stage introduces a ball. Place it on the tee. As you follow the same arm-and-shoulder-moving step, keep the backswing abbreviated. The hands go no higher than the hips. As the ball leaves the clubface at impact and the arms straighten, it is very important that you "freeze" your arms-extended position for a full five-second count. You should perform the four stages of this drill at slow, half and three-quarter speeds.

During this critical learning period, Natural Golf urges you to become acutely aware of the clubface's square relationship to the target. Also take note of other traits of the Natural Golf swing—how both feet are flat on the ground, how you are balanced and how your body rotation is virtually nonexistent.

After you strike the ball, hold your position and check the following:

a. The palm of the right hand should be pointed at the target.

b. The right arm should be straight.

c. The left knee should be flexed forward and the head should be back over the right knee.

d. The knees, hips and shoulders should be parallel to the target line.

Do 10 repetitions of this drill without interruption. It is quite useful if you have a "learner's caddie" re-tee the golf ball between repetitions.

In stage 4, address the ball on a tee in the Straight Line Setup (5), make an abbreviated backswing (6), swing into impact (7) and freeze with the arms extended for a count of five (8).

Fourth Stage

5 **6** **7** **8**

Right-hand-only chip-shot drill

A second way to learn Natural Golf's striking action is the "right-hand-only chip-shot" drill. Follow these steps:

1. Hold the club in the right hand in Natural Golf's Straight Line Setup.

2. Stand with the ball in the center of your stance with the knees, hips and shoulders parallel to the target line.

3. Swing the club back and fully extend or "cock" the right wrist until the shaft is parallel to the ground.

4. Holding that extended position, or wrist angle, of the right hand, move the club forward to the ball and hit a short shot of five to 10 yards. It is very important that you maintain the angle of the wrist extension in this drill.

After you strike the ball, hold your position and check the following:

a. The palm of the right hand should be pointed at the target.

b. The right arm should be straight and there should be a straight line from the head of the club through its handle, up the left knee and hip to the shoulder.

c. The left knee should be flexed forward and the head should be back over the right knee.

d. The knees, hips and shoulders should be parallel to the target line.

> "Your shots are more predictable. You have fewer penalty strokes."
>
> —Randy Zwetzig, Colorado

1

With your right hand holding the club in the Natural Palm Grip and with the ball in the center of your stance, address the ball in the Straight Line Setup with the wrist in the proper extended or cocked position (1). Swing the club back so the shaft is parallel to ground (2), then swing into impact and maintain the wrist-extension angle (3).

Square hips at impact drill

Another learning exercise that Natural Golf holds equally important to the ball-striking drills is the "square hips at impact" drill. For a conventional golfer converting to Natural Golf, this may prove to be the biggest learning challenge. The drill is designed to reduce the hip and torso rotation that is so pronounced in most renditions of the conventional golf swing.

Begin by standing at the ball in the Natural Golf Setup position. Drop the club and put your right hand on your right hip while allowing your left arm to drop to your side.

Next, push your right hip straight toward your left hip just a few inches. When you move your hips correctly, your left knee will naturally bend out toward the toes of your left foot.

Once you get there, your lower body has arrived at the Natural Golf impact position. Hold it. Let your subconscious understand it. It is not an exaggerated position. Your upper body has remained stable and in its original position, though slightly lower.

Slowly and gradually begin a rocking motion

from that impact position to the start position, and go back and forth without a club.

This sideways hip move, when coordinated with the proper Natural Golf swing, is not a big movement but is very strong.

Now, add a club to the exercise. Go to the impact position, then rock back and forth again as you did without the club.

Next, move the club back to the "top of your half-swing" position, then coordinate the forward swing with your forward rocking motion. You should reach the arms-extended impact position at the same time your hips slide and your left knee bends toward the toes of your left foot.

Finally, add a ball to a tee and strike it. Have your "learner's caddie" re-tee more balls as you perform the drill in slow motion.

Repeat all three drills in the early stages of learning the Natural Golf System and keep coming back to them on a regular basis during your first year of Natural Golfing. The drills can be performed at slow, half and three-quarter speeds, and with all clubs. Natural Golf strongly urges you, however, to do most of your drill work with a wedge or a 9-iron.

Without a club, take a Natural Golf Setup position (1), then push the right hip toward the left so the left knee naturally bends (2). Now with a club in your hands, repeat the sideways hip movement from address to impact in a back-and-forth rocking motion (3-4).

Power Dial

Because of the efficiency of the Natural Golf swing, with its Straight Line, Square Tracking delivery of the clubhead to the ball at impact, you are going to hit the ball far. You are going to increase your distance. Natural Golf defines this phenomenon as its Power Dial.

The Power Dial is in the subconscious. It invariably kicks in when you come to trust that the Natural Golf swing will repeatedly bring the clubface squarely back to the ball on a regular basis. As that trust becomes a permanent fixture in your Natural Golf personality, you begin, without realizing it, to strike the ball with more muscular and coor-dinated energy. As the Natural Golf Power Dial turns itself up, you hit the ball farther.

Accomplished conventional golfers who become Natural Golfers say the Power Dial turns on when they come to trust that Natural Golf's Square Tracking clubface will produce a straighter shot. They subconsciously become more aggressive as they come to realize that wild and crooked shots are less likely.

If you are in that category and are considering changing to Natural Golf, you should pay special attention to Chuck Hogan's important help in this book *(page 68)*. It specifically deals with the mental issues involved in making changes in your game like this.

"I'm knocking the hell out of the ball. . . I am a 57-year-old man and I am outdriving these kids. It's driving my son crazy."

—Herb Perlin, Virginia

As you begin to trust the Natural Golf swing, you will subconsciously turn up your Power Dial.

PRACTICING NATURAL GOLF

Practicing Natural Golf is one of the real rewards of the system. We would never say that practice is unnecessary. You do need to practice. Natural Golfers, however, find that more of their practice time is of high quality—more focused on shotmaking than swing mechanics—than their conventional playing friends' practice.

How can we say that?

Conventional players' primary practice goal is the coordination and timing of the five different rotary motions that comprise their more complex swings.

The fewer moving parts of the Natural Golf System means you have fewer maintenance "check points" to keep in tune. Thus, in the time that you can allocate to practice, you will spend less of it recovering coordination and timing.

Because the Natural Golf motion is such an efficient way to swing, you can spend more time practicing the finer points of play. For example, practicing from difficult lies and on different terrain is always smart. Practicing a preshot routine that becomes second nature on the course is a high priority.

Creating fantasy play conditions is good. So are opportunities to practice on different grass textures, from rough and in varying weather conditions.

Alignment practice is a must.

But, most important to any practice is target selection. Always choose a target. On every practice shot, you should carry a mental image of where and how you want your ball to fly or roll or bounce.

> *"I don't feel that I have to practice for hours and hours. I can go out and maybe hit just a couple of balls to loosen up and then go right out on the course."*
>
> —Mike Mullroy, New Jersey

The luxury of practicing all of those "quality" elements of your shots is one of Natural Golf's gifts to you. Natural Golf gives you more time for quality practice and perhaps even more time to play because its fewer moving parts require less servicing. That is especially valuable for the crowd of players whose passion for golf exceeds their available leisure hours.

The Natural Golfer can focus more on shotmaking than swing mechanics on the practice tee.

SHOTMAKING & NATURAL GOLF

New Natural Golfers ask a lot of questions about specific areas of golf that deserve attention here. What Natural Golf's dramatic innovation has done is greatly improve upon an existing method. We have not reinvented golf, just as we haven't reinvented the wheel. What Natural Golf has done is devise a major, major improvement.

The ball-flight physics laws that have been ably described in competent conventional studies still apply to Natural Golf shots.

• The path of the swing and the angle of the clubface at impact with the ball still determine the side spin on the ball that produces hooks, draws, fades and slices.

• The steepness of the path and the angle of the clubface still affect how high a ball will fly.

• Where the ball is positioned in the stance still affects the trajectory of its flight.

Aiming or alignment is a subject dear to Natural Golf. We place special emphasis on learning proper alignment, but the fundamentals are pretty much the same as with conventional golf.

First, you create an imaginary straight line from your target to a spot in front of your ball to a spot behind your ball. You put your clubface on that line, perpendicular to it and slightly behind the ball.

Then you create another imaginary straight line exactly parallel to the first line and stand on it, keeping your feet, knees, hips and shoulders parallel to the first line, too.

The most common visual image to aid you in understanding proper alignment is of a golfer standing on a railroad track. One rail is the line for the club and ball, and the other rail is the line for the feet and body.

The reason Natural Golf harps on alignment or aiming is because we know that Natural Golfers are likely to hit the ball much straighter than conventional golfers are.

Sometimes when players new to Natural Golf are aimed poorly, they still hit the ball in the woods or rough or water. But they hit it straight into the trouble instead of curving it there. When you couple proper aiming and the Natural Golf swing, the strong, straight result lets the method speak for itself. Loudly.

> ## "I haven't sliced a ball in over a year."
> —Eric Squires, Maine

> **For proper alignment, imagine a railroad track: The clubface and ball are on the rail that goes to the target; your feet and body align with the other rail.**

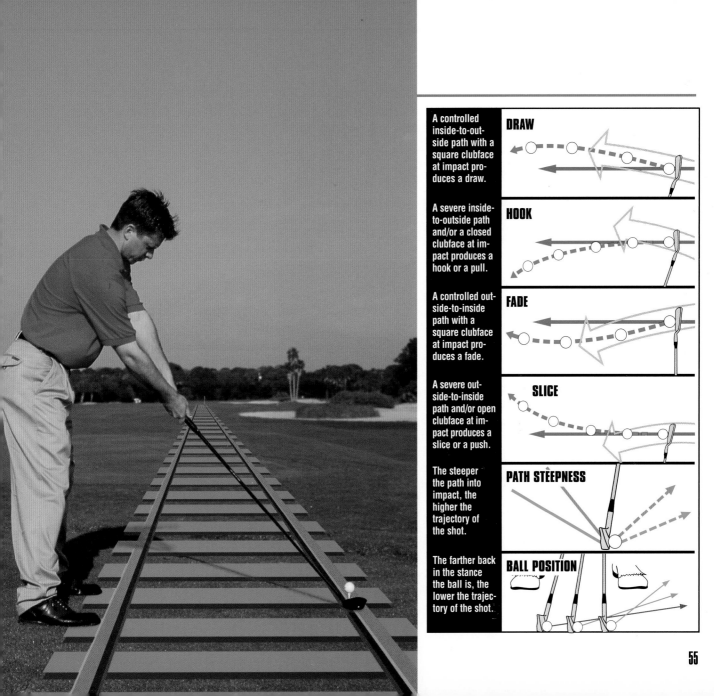

A controlled inside-to-outside path with a square clubface at impact produces a draw.

DRAW

A severe inside-to-outside path and/or a closed clubface at impact produces a hook or a pull.

HOOK

A controlled outside-to-inside path with a square clubface at impact produces a fade.

FADE

A severe outside-to-inside path and/or open clubface at impact produces a slice or a push.

SLICE

The steeper the path into impact, the higher the trajectory of the shot.

PATH STEEPNESS

The farther back in the stance the ball is, the lower the trajectory of the shot.

BALL POSITION

THE SHORT GAME & NATURAL GOLF

All things being equal, one of golf's greatest thrills is to bash the ball to the outer limits of our capabilities. As discussed, Natural Golf's Square Tracking swing path instills a confidence in Natural Golfers that subconsciously makes them crank up their internal Power Dials and hit the ball far.

The reality of golf life, though, is that all things are very rarely equal. You can hit the ball farther than Tom, but Dick can hit it farther than you.

The great equalizer is golf's finesse game—the short game. It is where warts become beauty marks and where strength, stature and brawn don't count. It is played within 100 yards of the green—the area where every player can swing at less than full strength.

And any time a golfer swings at less than full strength, there are no physical limitations on the quality of the shot. You can play short shots as well as Arnie, Nancy, Jack, Tiger, Annika and Moe.

A complete golfer respects the entirety of the game. Smart golfers identify their personal physical shortcomings and know intuitively to play within them. There are no physical limitations to short-game excellence.

It is golf's short game that often dilutes the glamour of the behemoth's long-flying shots by creating its own enviable territory—a lower score.

The short game is an area where even stars on the PGA, Senior PGA, LPGA and overseas tours have been known to adopt methods that mirror Natural Golf's Square Tracking techniques.

Many tour stars adjust their grips for shots close to the green. They move the grip of the club into the meaty part of the right hand and position the handle parallel to the right forearm. That is Natural Golf.

Natural Golfers find, once again, that the confidence that Square Tracking instills is probably the greatest asset they have. Knowing that the blade of the club will move the ball consistently on the target line and remain on that line is invaluable. That knowledge allows you to focus only on target and trajectory, so you can concentrate on the feel and velocity of the short stroke you are about to make.

Accomplished Natural Golfers, including Moe Norman, describe a feeling of "passive hands" through the impact area of all Natural Golf shots. They feel as though their hands do not participate in the striking action. It is a perception.

It is a good perception, especially in pitching

"I found definite improvement in all my short irons. I can really get accurate. I have even hit some pins, which is something I've never done before."

—Ben Heino, New York

and chipping. Try to feel as though your forearms assume a leadership role on the short shots. Resist conscious thought of your hands and of release in pitch and chip shots.

The notion of "passive hands" and "moving forearms," combined with the stability of the club in the palm of the right hand, encourages a stable left wrist in the impact area. Golf's Grinch, which ruins most short shots, is the collapsing left wrist during impact. It usually occurs when you consciously attempt to scoop the ball into the air by striking with the right hand.

Natural Golf teaches the short game from the fringe of the green—chipping—back to the fairway—pitching. Many of the Natural Golf elements of those two parts of the short game also apply to sand shots and putting.

For many golfers, not just Natural ones, the key to a better short game is a Square Tracking clubface.

1

CHIPPING

Chipping—low-flying and long-rolling short-game shots, usually from close to the green—is a cross between pitching and putting. Most good chippers attempt to land the ball just on the green and get it rolling as soon as possible.

The real art to chipping is club selection. Club choice is dictated by how the ball lies on the ground and how far it must travel in the air to land on the putting surface. Experiment with different clubs to learn which work best in different chipping situations.

Once again, Natural Golf's Straight Line Set-up produces a confidence-building Square Tracking clubface through chipping's tiny impact zone. You regularly see that setup emulated by many pro-tour stars, who purposely adjust their grips to allow it to occur. Look at the stars who use their putting grips when they chip. They definitely are Square Tracking.

For Natural Golf chip shots, follow these fundamentals:

• Choose a club that fits the situation.

• Use the Natural Palm Grip while choking down on the club and assume the Straight Line Setup.

• Narrow the stance so the feet are close together and align the stance slightly open to, or left of, the target line.

• Position the ball toward the back of your stance so the hands are in front of the ball. This puts the right wrist in an extended, or cocked, position, eliminating the need to further cock the wrist on the backswing on most shots.

"It's a good system. Under a lot of pressure, it holds up."

—Gene Forbes, Virginia

2

•Distribute your weight toward the left side, so your shoulders are tilted in a way that allows a more upright backswing and a steeper angle into the ball on the downswing.

• On the backswing, swing your arms far enough back to hit the ball the proper distance.

• On the downswing, maintain the extended, or cocked, angle of the right wrist through impact. Keep the hands "passive."

• Maintain a firm left wrist through the impact zone.

• Keep the palm of the right hand going toward the target.

• Imagine the trajectory and roll of the chip you intend to make and let the loft of the club lift the ball into the air.

• Allow the chip-shot swing to occur in the same subconscious way Natural Golf full shots do, while your mind is thinking about your target. Natural Golf's Square Tracking will enable you to forget about mechanics and concentrate on the feel and distance of chip shots.

The Natural Golf chipping stroke: The extended or cocked wrist position at address (1) should be maintained through impact (2).

PITCHING

Pitching is the name of a variety of short-game shots that fly through the air on a high arc and land on the green, then roll varying lengths to the hole. Most pitch shots are hit with wedges. Some specialty pitch shots, such as low-flying shots against strong wind, are better hit with other less-lofted clubs.

The Natural Golf pitch shot is in many ways a longer version of the Natural Golf chip shot. Experiment with your different wedges—pitching, sand and lob—to learn which work best in different pitching situations.

> **"I can use a 9-iron and hit all my balls within probably a 10-foot radius of each other."**
>
> **—Katie Zwetig, Colorado**

For Natural Golf pitch shots, follow these fundamentals.

• Use the Natural Palm Grip and assume the Straight Line Setup.

• Narrow the stance slightly.

• Evenly distribute your weight between both feet and position the ball for a wedge *(see page 29)*. Be sure the right wrist is in an extended, or cocked, position.

• On the backswing, swing your arms far enough back to hit the ball the proper distance. On longer swings, allow the right wrist to extend, or cock, a little more than the pre-set extension of the Straight Line Setup.

• On the downswing, maintain the extended, or cocked, angle of the wrist through impact. Keep the hands "passive."

• Keep the palm of the right hand going

1

toward the target.

• Maintain a firm left wrist through the impact zone. On higher shots, allow the hands to release a little after impact.

• Learn to control distances by the length of the backswing. Imagine the dial of a clock. Determine, for example, the different distances of sand wedge shots when your backswing goes to 9 o'clock, to 10 o'clock, to 11 o'clock and to 12 o'clock.

2

The Natural Golf pitching stroke: From the Straight Line Setup position (1), take a short backswing (2), then swing through impact with a firm left wrist (3).

3

• Imagine the trajectory and roll of the shot you intend to hit.

• Allow the pitch-shot swing to occur in the same subconscious way Natural Golf full shots do, while your mind is thinking about your target. Natural Golf's Square Tracking will enable you to forget about mechanics and concentrate on the feel and distance of your pitch shots.

GREENSIDE SAND SHOTS

Playing sand shots near the green is a real dilemma for learners. They have great difficulty accepting the concept that you are not supposed to hit the ball! But once you understand what occurs during a sand shot, the mystery goes away.

You are supposed to hit the sand first, about an inch or two or more behind the ball. The sand acts like a pillow. It cushions the force of the impact of the clubface. That allows you to make an assertive swing through the sand on such a short shot, and the ball flies out on that displaced pillow or cushion of sand. A tentative swing in a sand bunker often gets stuck in the sand. The ball moves only slightly, leaving it in the bunker to be played again.

A close-up view of the bounce on the sole of a sand wedge.

The first object of sand play is to get out of the bunker. Because bunkers are depressions, the ball needs to be hit into the air. Only on rare occasions will a rolling ball get out of a bunker.

Sand wedges are built with plenty of loft to give your shot the necessary height to fly out of the bunker. They also are built with a sole feature—bounce—that helps keep the club from digging too deeply into the sand. When you utilize the special properties of the sand wedge in combination with the correct fundamentals described below, you will make successful Natural Golf greenside sand shots.

As in pitching and chipping, ball trajectory and spin affect the roll of sand shots. Ball position, swing-path steepness and intensity of impact affect ball trajectory and spin. Repetition and experimentation with those elements is the foundation of the sand game learning process.

For Natural Golf greenside sand-bunker shots, follow these fundamentals:

• Use a sand wedge.

• Assume the Natural Golf Straight Line Set-up, opening the face of the club. To open the clubface, rotate the grip in your hands; do not reposition your hands.

• Take a stable stance. Make sure your footing is secure in the sand. Align your normal stance slightly open to, or left of, the landing area you choose.

• Choose the "size of the sand cushion" by picking a grain of sand to hit that is an inch or two behind the ball.

• Make sure your forearms take a leadership role and make an assertive swing that finishes well past the ball. Let your hands be active in the impact area.

• Vary the flexibility of your left wrist from firm to "cupped," depending on the lie and the desired height of the shot. A firm left wrist will produce a lower shot with less spin. A "cupped" wrist will produce a higher shot with more spin.

• Control the distance with the length and speed of the swing. A short, slow swing with a

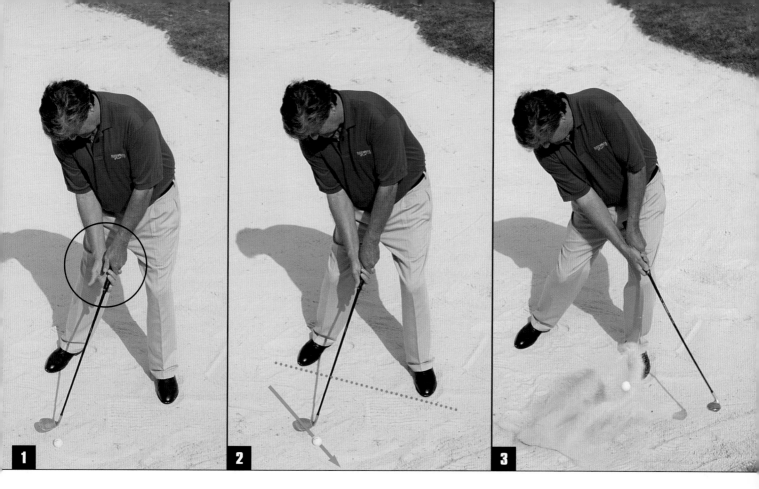

1

2

3

cupped wrist will result in a short, lofted, spinning shot. A longer, faster swing with a firm wrist will produce a lower, longer-rolling shot with less spin.

• Restrict your lower body movement and your foot movement.

• Allow the sand-shot swing to occur in the same subconscious way Natural Golf full shots do, while your mind is thinking about your target. Natural Golf's Square Tracking will enable you to forget about mechanics and concentrate on the feel and distance of bunker shots.

You can play a short flop, or lob, shot from grass using your lob wedge or sand wedge by using the same fundamentals as a Natural Golf greenside sand shot. Play the ball forward in your stance, rotate the handle in your hands clockwise to open the clubface and make a long, slow swing. At impact, allow the left wrist to cup as the right hand accelerates. Finish with the clubface facing the sky. The flop shot is difficult to repeat on a consistent basis. Use it only as a last resort.

The Natural Golf sand shot: Rotate the wedge in your hands (1) to open the clubface in the Straight Line Setup. Align your stance slightly left of the target line (2) and pick a spot in the sand an inch or two behind the ball. Make an assertive swing through that spot so the ball flies out on a cushion of sand (3).

PUTTING

Putting is the best evidence that Natural Golf's Square Tracking club path is the most ideal approach to hitting a golf ball.

Many serious competitors in the world of golf, when they putt, use Natural Golf's fundamental Straight Line Setup, the setup that runs the handle of the golf club through the palm of the right hand and parallel to the right forearm.

The popular reverse-overlap conventional putting grip begins by putting the putter in the right hand the way Natural Golf teaches you to hold all of the clubs. That allows Square Tracking to occur. And in putting, where precise accuracy and distance control are mandatory, Square Tracking is the choice of millions of players.

By placing the putter in the right hand in the Natural Palm Grip, you simplify the process of aligning the putterface. You simply rely on natural instinct to aim the palm, and thus the putterface, at the target. It's as natural as if you were tossing a softball underhand, a motion in which you do not worry about alignment. The

When you position the palm against the trademarked square Natural Golf putter grip, the putterface and the palm will move in the same direction.

Natural Golf putting stroke helps eliminate the tension and anxiety created by alignment worries.

In putting, the Rules of Golf allow Natural Golf to further enhance the Square Tracking concept by installing square grips on our putters. The trademarked square Natural Golf putter grip is precisely aligned with the clubface. When you put the flat surface of the putter against the palm of the hand, it insures that the face of the club and palm move in the same direction—eliminating doubt and encouraging confidence that the two are working in concert.

Accepting the positive effects of Square Tracking putting as a given, there are two variations of the putting stroke that successful golfers use.

The first, and more popular, is the pendulum stroke. It features movement mostly of the shoulders, and it minimizes arm and hand involvement.

The second is the piston stroke. In it, the right arm folds at the elbow on the backswing and straightens through the impact area on the forward swing.

> ## "The square grip has really improved my putting. It seems to make aiming automatic."
>
> —Len Wizmur, New Jersey

The pendulum stroke features shoulder movement and minimizes arm and hand action (1-3). The piston stroke features a folding and unfolding of the right elbow (A-C).

PENDULUM

1 **2** **3**

PISTON

A **B** **C**

65

"The way you
hit the ball is an
easy confidence
builder."

—Tom Heenan, New Jersey

In the photography here, you can see that in the pendulum stroke, the putterhead moves off the line and then returns to it momentarily as the ball is struck. In the piston stroke, the putterhead stays on the intended target line throughout the stroke.

The benefit of the piston stroke is obvious, especially on putts of intermediate length—25 feet and less. On longer putts, however, the elbow fold of the piston stroke may become cumbersome, which likely explains the popularity of the shoulder-dominated pendulum method.

Your personal preference and experience with piston and pendulum putting strokes should influence your choice of method. Combinations of the methods are used by some very successful Natural Golfers.

For Natural Golf piston and pendulum putting strokes, follow these fundamentals:

• Place the handle of the putter in the palm of the right hand and extend it parallel to the right forearm. The right palm now should be parallel to the putterface.

• Position the left hand flat at address, in the putting grip of your choice (including left hand low), so it is parallel to the right palm. Extend, or cock, the right wrist to create an angle between the back of the hand and the back of the forearm.

• Stand comfortably so that your eyes are centered over the ball.

• Accelerate the putter through the striking area smoothly, resisting the temptation to consciously "hit" the ball with your hands.

• Maintain a firm left wrist and extended, or cocked, right wrist, through the entire putting stroke.

• Finish the stroke with the palm of the right hand directly on the target line.

• Keep your legs, torso and head still throughout the stroke.

Natural Golf recommends two putting drills:

1. Right-hand-only drill. Address the ball while standing 24 inches from the hole and holding the putter in just the right hand with the Natural Palm Grip. Putt the ball. Maintain the extension, or cocking, of the right wrist through the finish of the stroke and hold the finish position for five seconds. Check to see that your right palm is square to the target. Make sure the 24-inch putt is a straight one.

2. Eyes-on-the-hole drill. Address the ball while standing 10 feet from the hole and holding the putter in both hands with the right hand in the Natural Palm Grip. Keep your eyes on the hole and putt the ball. There is no need to look at the ball becaue you are relying on the natural ability of your right palm to aim the putter.

Repeat each drill 10 times.

Avoid thinking about putting mechanics during the actual stroke. See the target in your mind's eye. And remember, on breaking putts, the target is not always the hole. It may be the point at which the putt begins to curve.

Build a repeatable putting routine with practice. Then trust it.

The putterhead moves off the line in the backswing and follow-through of the pendulum stroke (1-3) while it stays on the target line throughout the piston stroke (A-C).

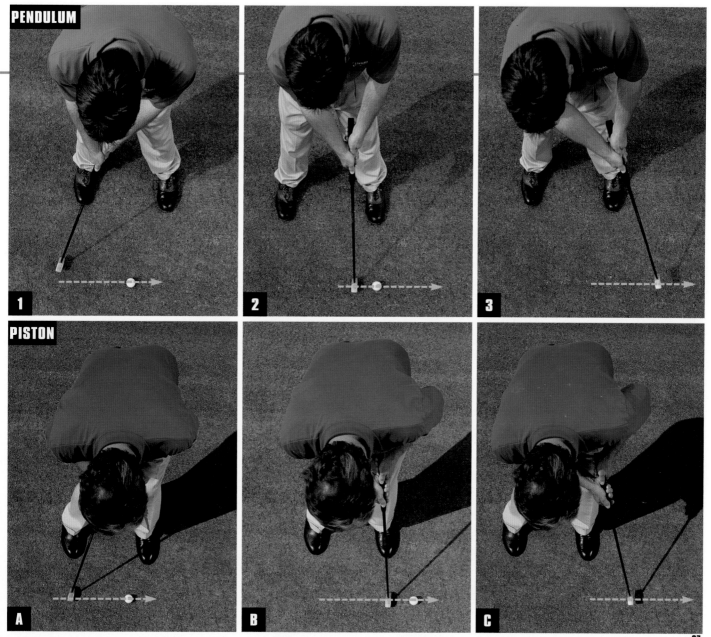

PENDULUM

1 2 3

PISTON

A B C

"Most people have draws or fades. My ball goes straight. There's no question that the ball is straighter than anybody else's. It's just phenomenal."

—Dave Hwalek, Virginia

TAKING NATURAL GOLF ONTO THE COURSE

Look at the target from behind the ball to form a mental picture of the ball's accurate flight.

The human part of golf—the fun, the exercise, the friendships, the time spent in fresh air, the thrill of hitting the ball far—is what makes it attractive to many who play. Yet when you get caught up in the heat of genuine competitive play, those same human elements can baffle you or simply disappear.

Natural Golf is proud to have Chuck Hogan help you manage your decision to learn to play Natural Golf. Hogan, who has coached such tour pros as Peter Jacobsen, Colleen Walker, John Cook, Johnny Miller, Raymond Floyd, Duffy Waldorf, David Ogrin and Cindy Rarick, is the founder of Sports Learning and Performance. His programs blend the mental and physical aspects of golf instruction.

Natural Golf's Moe Norman says, "The longest walk in golf is from the practice tee to the first tee." Millions agree.

Hogan now will help you take your Natural Golf game to the course—making that longest walk in golf shorter and more enjoyable.

From my perspective after playing, studying and teaching golf for 30 years, Natural Golf is clearly a better mousetrap. It is a better mousetrap because it is less complicated than any mousetrap made up to now in golf. This mousetrap has fewer moving parts, less chance of mechanical failure, and you don't have to guess whether or not the mouse is caught—you know it.

The Natural Golf method of propelling a golf ball is simpler to learn than the conventional method and, as such, it offers you ample opportunity to be free to play the game of golf instead of playing golf mechanics. You can learn Natural Golf techniques comparatively quickly and then move on to playing golf. All of this depends on how you use your "mental" side.

Let me point out what I mean by the mental side. It is when your conscious thinking is involved with the grip, the positioning of the club in the backswing, and the balanced position at the finish of the swing, etc. By definition then, your focus on the target, its distance and the flight of the ball is compromised.

> "It just seems much easier. You just get up there and hit it. Before, I was thinking about all the things I needed to do."
>
> —Faith Beach, Viriginia

Chuck Hogan

The brain can send to your "physical" muscles only the images it is holding. So if your brain is holding images of golf mechanics, it cannot send the muscles what they need to direct the ball to the target. You physically get what you think. So as you approach Natural Golf, be careful of what you ask. You can make an even better mousetrap dysfunctional for catching mice.

Confusion is the great killer of golf scores and enjoyment of golf. Certainly there are some things to be learned in the preparation for playing golf. Mentally you do need to grasp the techniques for holding the club, aiming the club and using the club. But these are the pieces that you master in preparation to play golf. You learn them, master them and then move on to playing golf.

Golf is the activity of moving "this" ball to "that" target. It is a dot to dot to dot game. The clubface has a dot on it, the ball has a dot on it and the target is a dot. Golf is connecting the dots. Mentally, this is about all that is necessary when you are playing golf.

When you are learning what I call the pre-golf activities of grip, stance and posture, aim and alignment, and swing techniques, it is both desirable and necessary to be "mentally" (or consciously) focused on those activities—one chunk at a time. Follow this way of learning and you will stay mentally clear and precise. An absence of confusion at the mental level will manifest itself at the physical level in satisfying performance—you'll hit good shots.

The beauty of the Natural Golf motion is that its simplicity does not lend itself to the confusion built into the conventional golf swing. The Natural Golf motion is simple. Take the club and hit the back of the ball like you were hitting a nail with a hammer.

Confused? I doubt it. Yet I cannot count the number of gifted athletes I know who have been brought to their knees by the traditional learning process of the conventional golf motions.

By now, you are getting the idea that the "mental" stuff is the "physical" stuff. And you are absolutely correct. You are what you think. This is not a philosophical statement. It is a biological and organic fact of being a human being and a golfer. The fact is that you "feel" according to what you "think."

Now, here is the key question. How do you want to feel about the way you play golf? It is a question that you—not other golfers—should be in charge of answering. And the answer is important for anyone considering a transition from traditional golf to Natural Golf, or for any golf novice making a decision as to which method to use.

As you ponder your decision about playing Natural Golf, you might think of or hear the question phrased a different way. Many people are compelled to ask: "So, if Moe Norman was so great, why didn't he win a lot of tournaments and why haven't I heard of him?"

One answer is that he got beat up pretty badly for being different. There is a cliché that is very true and appropriate to golfers. What is new is not acceptable. What is acceptable is not new.

Moe Norman's childhood determined that he would be far less than an outgoing social being. Like many individuals in this position, he was reclusive, resourceful and inventive. He retreated to unknown fields to strike golf balls. Perhaps it was the enlightenment of a savant or perhaps it was the stubbornness of a mule, but Moe Norman found a way to strike a ball that was superior in simplicity to the known, accepted method.

When Moe Norman took his skills to the competitive course, he was brutally ridiculed for how he looked, talked and hit a ball. His successes were many in his native Canada despite the obstacles. When he came to play in the United States, he was even more castigated by the good old boys of golf. Still, Moe Norman became a legend in the inner circles of golf, and he has all the credentials to prove the validity of his method from those years in competitive golf in Canada. Moe Norman's swing was new and it was not accepted. Ultimately, it will be fully accepted but not new.

This has everything to do with you. Taking up the Natural Golf method will make you both a pioneer and a golfer who stands out.

Your attitude will largely determine your potential to both play and enjoy the game to your satisfaction. If you are "mentally" ready to run your own brain, then the Natural Golf method can be your shortest and most durable route to a better game. You are the one in charge of what is better.

This book presents the learning process one step at a time. You simply need to follow each step, one small chunk at a time, employing a cycle of imprint (grasping the instructions), repetition (practice) and habituation (making Natural Golf fundamentals a habit). Within days, weeks at the outside, you will be executing the Natural Golf motion consistently and proficiently.

The next step is preparing to actually hit golf shots. The score that you produce is a function of your ability (or inability) to:

1. Aim.
2. Center the hit of the ball in the middle of the clubface.
3. Propel the ball the correct distance.

In the learning process, the above is the correct order. In the scoring process, the order reverses. The correct distance is the most important element of scoring. Your comprehension of the significance of these scoring factors will determine how you allocate your practice time.

The motion used in Natural Golf lends

> ## "I am having fun every time I play golf."
>
> —Ken Williamson, South Carolina

itself to accurate aim. Because the Natural Golf swing is a single-axis movement and the hit is made with a square clubface, your "mental" picture is simply straight. You look at your target from behind the ball on the straight line to the hole. "Mentally" you see a straight flight. Your subconscious will point your clubface at the target and put your body perpendicular to the clubface. Much of this process is compromised in the conventional swing because of the two-axis, rotating clubface inherent to the motion. With Natural Golf your aim will be accurate and automatic.

By definition, the Natural Golf motion centers the hit in the middle of the clubface. The equipment of Natural Golf defines and gives clarity to the center of the clubface. The striking motion of Natural Golf resembles that of hitting a nail on its head. You will find that it is very clear whether or not you hit the nail on the head.

To hit the ball to the target you must do two things: You must hit the ball in the right direction and hit it the right distance. You have already incorporated the direction in the learning of the aim and swing. All that is left is accurate distance response. Distance can be learned but it cannot be taught. To repeat, it is the most important part of scoring, but it cannot be taught. It can only be learned.

You can learn a lot about distance control by practicing the short game. The short game is the largest part of your score, comprising 63 percent of your stroke total. And the short game is mostly about the distance component—the "supreme" mental game.

As you are imprinting, repeating and habituating the full Natural Golf motion, also please take the opportunity to putt and chip. Roll short, long and medium distance putts. Roll uphill, downhill and sidehill putts. Roll putts on slow, fast and medium surfaces. Learn to stop the ball at specific distances in all situations when putting and chipping. Nothing is more mental or will save you more strokes.

Learn the pitch, sand and specialty shots in the same cycle of competence as you learned the full motion. That should be easy because, in the Natural Golf motion, these shots are essentially smaller versions of the full motion. They are not new and separate motions, as they often are taught in the conventional method.

When you have put together the pre-golf pieces, you are ready to play golf. Mentally you have separated mechanics from targeting. On the course (and on the range once the pieces are together), you are ready to adhere to *the law*.

The law is: When you are thinking mechanics, there is no target. When there is a target in mind, you do not consider mechanics.

As you religiously adhere to *the law*, you eliminate mental confusion, ambiguity and frustration. You do not compromise your perfectly good brain by mixing agendas and splitting your attention.

On the course, golf is: "This ball to that target." Imagine the desired shot from behind the ball, viewing down the target line. Hold that image as you move into position. Align the clubface. Align your body, settling into comfort. Take one more look at the target for distance reference only. Execute.

Celebrate your good shots. Look at your bad shots once and once only. Replay a "good" shot in your mind and celebrate the replay.

Celebrate the good with more intensity and duration than you berate the bad. The reality is that the golfing society expects destructive expression as the norm and considers celebration of success as deviant. This is not nature. The true Natural Golfer would celebrate the good and learn from the bad.

Does choosing to be an expressively happy, confident golfer necessarily mean that you are going to hit every shot perfect? Absolutely not! It means that you have the chance to hit great shots over and over again.

The Natural Golf motion is easy to learn, easy to execute and easy to repeat. Learn the motion. Next, apply your attention to the ball and to striking it in the middle of the clubface. Then put your full attention on the ball going to the target, working on the accuracy of distance. Congratulate yourself for completing the process.

Now, move on to the game. The game is between your ears. Play more than you practice, congratulate yourself for every good shot when it occurs and, as you drive home from the course, remember every good shot that you experienced that day.

In short, play the game!

OTHER ASPECTS OF NATURAL GOLF

EQUIPMENT

Natural Golf's Straight Line Setup and Square Tracking path are ideally performed with equipment that has physical characteristics that support them.

The most obvious difference between Natural Golf's clubs and conventional clubs is in the grips. A Natural Golfer requires clubs with grips that are thicker than conventional ones. They also should not be tapered. Why? Because a Natural Golfer holds the grip in the meaty part of the hand—the palm—while a conventional player holds the grip almost exclusively in the fingers.

When a Natural Golfer plays with the narrow, tapered handles of conventional equipment, he may notice a tendency for the clubhead to feel as if it is twisting off square at impact with the ball.

A less obvious but required equipment change is in the lie angle of the club. The effective lie angle of conventional clubs needs adjustment to accommodate the more upright configuration of Natural Golf's Straight Line Setup.

Fitting a Natural Golfer to the proper equipment involves many elements. Natural Golf fitting professionals will consider your stature, strength and swing traits when devising their equipment recommendations for you.

The Natural Golf Corporation sells custom-fitted equipment that it considers ideal for its method. The company's renowned designer, Robert Lukasiewicz, has set the center of gravity of Natural Golf's perimeter-weighted clubheads slightly higher than where you find it in conventional equipment.

When the clubface impacts the ball, the higher center of gravity tends to produce a more solid hit. It transfers more energy from the clubhead to the ball.

A detailed description of Natural Golf equipment and its fitting requirements is available on request from Natural Golf Corporation. Call toll free: 888-NAT-GOLF.

HEALTH ISSUES

Many Natural Golfers—especially those with back problems—report to Natural Golf that its system does not cause them as much discom-fort as the twisting and rotating required by conventional methods.

Intuitively, Natural Golf expects that its swing's reduced rotations put less stress on the body than the rotations of a conventional swing. Fueled by that expectation, Natural Golf is working with qualified medical and therapeutic organizations in hopes of being able to support its intuition with reliable professional opinions. Until Natural Golf is able to report reliable information on the subject, it has no official position regarding the system's bodily risks or benefits.

Natural Golf's custom-fitted clubs feature clubheads with an adjusted lie angle and thick, untapered grips designed for the Natural Palm Grip.

WHAT OTHERS ARE SAYING ABOUT
NATURAL GOLF

Natural Golf has received media coverage in many major publications.

MEDIA

Golf Digest's December 1995 issue, which devoted considerable space and a foldout cover to Moe Norman and the Natural Golf method, catapulted both to prominence. Before then, Moe Norman enjoyed prominence only among very ardent students of the game, and Natural Golf was basically an unknown entity. That golf media breakthrough sent a signal to legitimate media that Natural Golf was a story worthy of attention.

Subsequently, *The New York Times*, *The Wall Street Journal*, *Men's Journal*, The Discovery Channel, ESPN and The Golf Channel all have reported in-depth stories on the Natural Golf Method and Moe Norman.

NATURAL GOLFERS

A Lifetime of Better Golf? Isn't that a presumptuous claim?

Not to hear Natural Golfers tell it.

As you've worked through this book, you have noticed quotations in the margins that have been attributed to amateur Natural Golfers.

They are excerpts from unrehearsed taped telephone conversations with Natural Golfers who agreed to be interviewed by journalist John Torsiello, whom Natural Golf commissioned to conduct the interviews.

GOLF PROFESSIONALS

The professional golf community is beginning to accept Natural Golf as a legitimate method of playing golf. Golf Digest Schools' John Elliott commented in an earlier work that he believed it was his responsibility as a golf professional to consider Natural Golf as a valid way to play the game.

PGA Tour veteran Ken Ellsworth and Asian and Canadian Tour competitor Todd Graves lead a contingent of professionals who play and teach Natural Golf.

In addition, the Professional Golfers' Association of America—the teaching pro organization—allows its members to acquire continuing education annual credits should a member attend one of Natural Golf's educational presentations.

Natural Golf is developing a PGA colleagues program that will encourage club professionals to become qualified in Natural Golf or provide PGA members convenient access to Natural Golf instruction.

WHAT'S NEXT
FOR YOU & NATURAL GOLF?

Natural Golf's instructors are ready to help you.

Learning Natural Golf begins with owning this book. If you are able to follow and perform the method as we describe and demonstrate it here, you will succeed.

The promise of Natural Golf is realized in proportions equal to your effort and the athleticism you were born with. Are you the next Moe Norman? Maybe, but likely not.

We do know that Natural Golf will maximize your golf potential. By now you know why we are comfortable making that promise to you.

You may accelerate and insure the process by learning directly from a qualified Natural Golf instructor. There are several options. The first step is to call Natural Golf world headquarters at 888-NAT-GOLF.

Our counselors and professionals will outline the available Natural Golf educational opportunities. The headquarters staff works with each Natural Golfer and sculpts an individual learning program. Your budget, skills,

goals and location will affect the plan the staff devises with you.

Together you may choose a plan that includes travel to one of our permanent Natural Golf learning centers, which are always staffed by a Natural Golfmaster and Natural Golf Professional. Or you may find that a qualified and certified Natural Golf instructor is located near you.

Demonstrations and clinics, one-, three- and five-day schools, executive camps and private lessons are just a few of the learning resources we may prescribe.

Whatever learning relationship you develop with us, we will support your efforts for the rest of your Natural life. As we grow, we will develop serious continuity support programs with our players.

Today, it is the telephone, the video camera and videotape, and even the Internet that we can put at your continuing disposal. In the future it could very well be live lessons through computers, linking hundreds of learners in scores of locations.

Our promise to support your Natural efforts will explore every technological edge that comes along. We are inspired to do that by your courage to help us make golf better.

THE FUTURE OF NATURAL GOLF

Natural Golfers are a proud lot. They appear to thrive on putting their discovery of a better way to play on display. We know some Natural

Golfers who wear a golf glove on the right hand like a merit badge.

A cult? Maybe, for now. But not for long, if Natural Golf has anything to do with it. Word of mouth is the best advertising. It is the backbone of Natural Golf's growth.

The promise of Natural Golf, and your interest in playing it, inspire the Natural Golf Corporation to pledge a hearty and continuing effort to helping you enjoy a lifetime of better golf.

Natural Golf will continue to nurture Natural Golfers with regular newsletters, tournaments, alerts to early technological developments, merchandise, learning discounts and other helpful programs we intend to develop.

We intend on insuring a lifetime of better golf for all our customers.

NATURAL GOLF
Happily Ever After

Tom Herskovits

Do you remember the intensity of "puppy love?"

That uncontrollable, totally distracting, emotional life experience that comes as a shocking surprise when you're not old enough to do anything about it?

If you do, you will understand the emotional rush I experienced when I struck my first real Natural Golf shot.

The difference between puppy love and Natural Golf is that today I am old enough to do something about it—so I convinced a group of my colleagues to make a major investment in Natural Golf.

My passion as Chairman of the Natural Golf Corporation is to introduce as many people as possible to the thrills and rewards of discovering a better way to play golf.

As a businessman, I know that your ability to judge the merits of this method will most assuredly favor us. Once you experience real Natural Golf shots, like me and thousands of other Natural Golfers, you will very likely begin a lifetime of better golf.

My job is to get you to have that experience. It is a labor of love, so to speak.

Golf came to me later in life. I took it up for business reasons. I worked at General Foods and golf was an integral part of its corporate culture.

The privilege that went with a management role there allowed me the further privilege of learning to play golf in the tradition-steeped environment of Winged Foot, the history-rich club in suburban New York.

Golf promptly captivated me. A zeal to play it well sent me to golf schools and seminars and lessons that quickly got me to a respectable 14 handicap. I stayed there—give or take an occasional hot or cold streak—for about 10 years. That is, until Natural Golf came into my life in the spring of 1997.

As I write this, it is the fall of 1997 and my handicap is 9! It has gone down about one stroke a month!

During my first summer of Natural Golf, I proudly teamed with my friend Jordan Katz to win our club's two-man championship.

Allow me to backtrack, please.

This is how I got Naturalized.

Dan Wallace, a colleague, gave me a heads-up on Natural Golf as I was headed out of town to Florida. The golf theory junkie in me wouldn't let me pass up another possible opportunity for improvement, so before I left I arranged to take a lesson at home from Natural Golf's Dave Woods.

The proverbial light bulb went off!

No, it exploded!

Conceptually, I was hooked, but I took that inaugural lesson indoors. I needed to see ball flight for proof. Hours later, I was in Florida's better weather, and outside.

At first I didn't hit the ball that well. I regrouped, reviewed and replayed the basic information that Dave had given me.

Over the next two days, this 14-handicapper shot two rounds in the 70's at the Boca Raton Resort. That did it.

My heart said go, go. My head said due diligence. So we did due diligence—business jargon for a thorough investigation.

The investigation was a clincher. We contacted 500 Natural Golfers and, for perspective, also called 100 conventional golfers. What we learned was stunning.

The typical Natural Golfer was upbeat and his or her golf had improved. Moreover, he told us he expected further improvement.

The typical golfer in our conventional control group was frustrated and had experienced little improvement in his golf game over time.

Stories of the promise of Natural Golf—better golf—spout willingly and enthusiastically from the lips and pens of happy Natural Golfers.

As Chairman of Natural Golf Corporation, I will apply my business energies to develop materials and equipment, and to recruit and train professionals, so that we can fulfill the promise of Natural Golf often and reliably.

We will keep our promise of a lifetime of better golf.

Natural Golfers will come to expect continuing and determined innovation from Natural Golf. We will embrace technology and employ every means at our disposal to insure that every Natural Golfer is satisfied with our efforts to teach, equip and support his or her Natural Golfing career.

As a Natural Golfer, my promise to you is to light your fire in a way that it hasn't been lit in years! Maybe since. . . .

Happy Natural Golfing,

Tom Herskovits
Chairman of the Board
Natural Golf Corporation